INSPIRE
HAIR FASHION FOR SALON CLIENTS

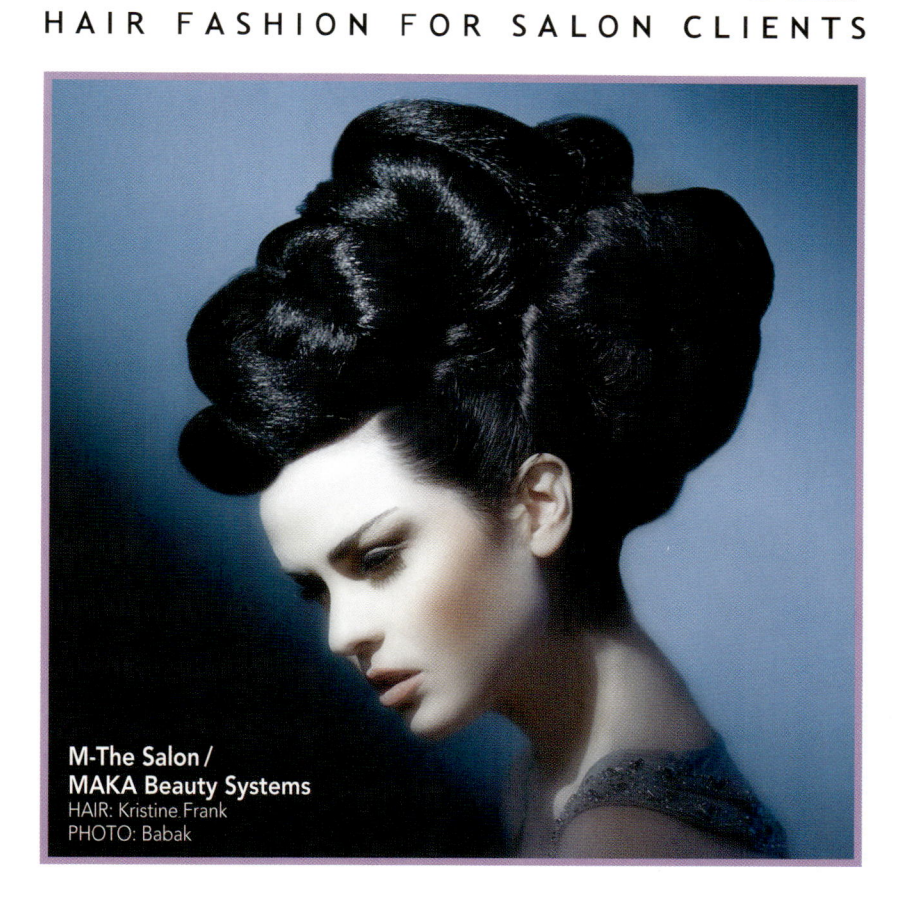

**M-The Salon /
MAKA Beauty Systems**
HAIR: Kristine Frank
PHOTO: Babak

INSPIRE
HAIR FASHION FOR SALON CLIENTS

Upstyles, Bridal & Special Occasion Hair

Table of Contents Volume 78

BRIDAL HAIRSTYLES
4-25

UPSTYLES
26-61

SPECIAL OCASSION HAIR
62-87

CELEBRITY HAIRSTYLES
88-95

Navii Salon Spa
HAIR: Tracey Stokes
MAKEUP: Jessica Sawicki
PHOTO: Jean Sweet

Navii Salon Spa
HAIR: Tracey Stokes
MAKEUP: Jessica Sawicki
PHOTO: Jean Sweet

Bridal Hair

Navii Salon Spa
HAIR: Tracey Stokes
MAKEUP: Jessica Sawicki
PHOTO: Jean Sweet

Salon 56
HAIR: Jessica Smith
MAKEUP: Gerine Coronado
PHOTO: Taggart Winterhalter for Purely Visual

Bridal Hair

7

Art of Hair
HAIR: Robin Dunn
MAKEUP: Jaime Queenin
PHOTO: Taggart Winterhalter
for Purely Visual

HAIR: Dean Roybal
MAKEUP: Lori Neapolitan
PHOTO: Michael S. Block

David Douglas Salon and Spa
HAIR: Vicki Maki
MAKEUP: Jaime Queenin
PHOTO: Taggart Winterhalter for Purely Visual

Bridal Hair

Navii Salon Spa
HAIR: Tracey Stokes
MAKEUP: Jessica Sawicki
PHOTO: Jean Sweet

Bridal Hair

Salon 56
HAIR: Stacy Klepach
MAKEUP: Stacy Klepach
PHOTO: Taggart Winterhalter
for Purely Visual

11

Pavé Nouveau
HAIR: Mandi Bevando
MAKEUP: Jaime Queenin
PHOTO: Taggart Winterhalter
for Purely Visual

Bridal Hair

Art of Hair
HAIR: Nicole Martin
MAKEUP: Sara Wayne
PHOTO: Taggart Winterhalter for Purely Visual

The Hair Station
HAIR: Jessica Feldpausch
COLOR: Jessica Feldpausch
MAKEUP: Jessica Feldpausch
PHOTO: Terri Feldpausch

13

Fantastic Sams
Rancho Cucamonga, CA
HAIR: Susana Perez
PHOTO: Taggart Winterhalter
for Purely Visual

Fantastic Sams
Huntington Beach, CA
HAIR: Nina Youkhana
PHOTO: Taggart Winterhalter
for Purely Visual

Bridal Hair

**Fantastic Sams
Huntington Beach, CA**
HAIR: Jennifer Newman
PHOTO: Taggart Winterhalter
for Purely Visual

**Fantastic Sams
Huntington Beach, CA**
HAIR: Wassan Sano
PHOTO: Taggart Winterhalter for Purely Visual

15

Bristles & Shears
HAIR: Suzanna Spears
MAKEUP: Suzanna Spears
PHOTO: Ed Soloman

**Fantastic Sams
Huntington Beach, CA**
HAIR: Wassan Sano
PHOTO: Taggart Winterhalter for Purely Visual

Hair International
HAIR: Elaina Holguin
MAKEUP: Elaina Holguin
PHOTO: Kristin Szczerbik

Bridal Hair

Salon Tekniques
HAIR: Marissa Toth
COLOR: Marissa Toth
MAKEUP: Marissa Toth
PHOTO: Scott Bryant

Salon De Christé
HAIR: Lori O'Reilly
MAKEUP: Kelly Simon
PHOTO: Heather Ramirez

Updo's Studio
HAIR: Amanda Gatewood
MAKEUP: Heather Still
PHOTO: Still Shots Photography

Bridal Hair

19

Rumors Salon and Spa
HAIR: Lejen Mae Opura
MAKEUP: Jennifer Schwartz
PHOTO: Denis J. Nally

Visible Changes
HAIR: Visible Changes
Artistic Team
MAKEUP: Visible Changes
Artistic Team
PHOTO: Dan Carter

Bridal Hair

Salon Secrets Spa & Wellness Retreat
HAIR: Jennifer Vargason
COLOR: Jennifer Vargason
MAKEUP: Dianna Fraim
PHOTO: Scott Bryant

John Amico Haircare & Jalyd Haircolor Parkview Shear Perfection
HAIR: Rhonda Murphy
COLOR: Rhonda Murphy
MAKEUP: Rhonda Murphy
PHOTO: Scott Bryant

Mosaic Day Spa & Salon
HAIR: Sandra Baliya
COLOR: Sandra Baliya
MAKEUP: Sandra Baliya
PHOTO: Jeff Tureaud

The Hair Loft
HAIR: Robin Cadrain
MAKEUP: Emily Redman
PHOTO: Artistic Images of Canton, LLC

Bridal Hair

23

Angeleah's
HAIR: Angeleah Daidone
MAKEUP: Patricia Daidone
PHOTO: Angeleah Daidone

Angeleah's
HAIR: Angeleah Daidone
MAKEUP: Patricia Daidone
PHOTO: Angeleah Daidone

The Salon Professionals
HAIR: Stephanie Boaz
PHOTO: Tina VanDerhoof

Bridal Hair

25

M-The Salon /
MAKA Beauty Systems
HAIR: Amy Freudenberg
MAKEUP: Mindy Hay
PHOTO: Matt Spencer

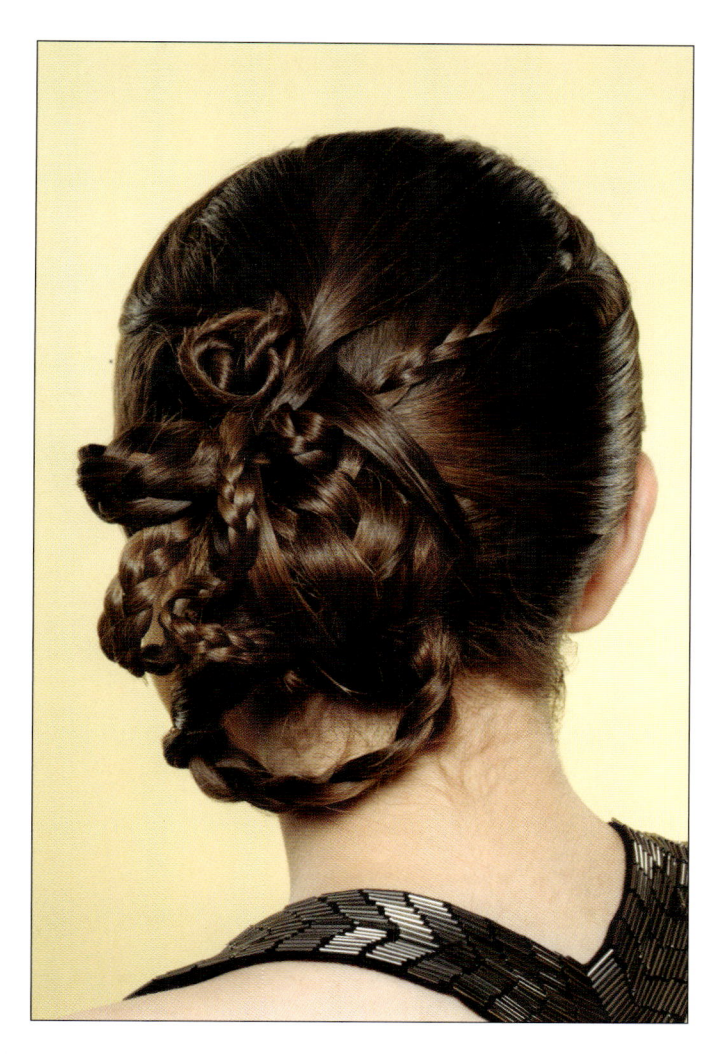

Pavé Nouveau
HAIR: Kathy Reed
MAKEUP: Sara Wayne
PHOTO: Taggart Winterhalter
for Purely Visual

Upstyles

Pavé Nouveau
HAIR: Kathy Reed
MAKEUP: Sara Wayne
PHOTO: Taggart Winterhalter
for Purely Visual

Upstyles

Martin Parsons
HAIR: Martin Parsons
MAKEUP: Cheryl Gushue
PHOTO: Dave Starrett
*Courtesy of Martin Parsons

Martin Parsons
HAIR: Martin Parsons
MAKEUP: Cheryl Gushue
PHOTO: Dave Starrett
*Courtesy of Martin Parsons

Cuttin Inn Salon & Spa
HAIR: Já Nice Estrada
MAKEUP: Já Nice Estrada
PHOTO: Taggart Winterhalter for Purely Visual

29

Pavé Nouveau
HAIR: Ashley Schmidt
MAKEUP: Tessa Stull
PHOTO: Taggart Winterhalter
for Purely Visual

HAIR: Dean Roybal
MAKEUP: Lori Neapolitan
PHOTO: Michael S. Block

Upstyles

The Art of Hair
HAIR: Robin Dunn
MAKEUP: Jamie Queenin
PHOTO: Taggart Winterhalter for Purely Visual

Pavé Nouveau
HAIR: Kathy Reed
MAKEUP: Sara Wayne
PHOTO: Taggart Winterhalter
for Purely Visual

Affinage
HAIR: Affinage Artistic Team
MAKEUP: Affinage Artistic Team
PHOTO: Paul Sargaison for Affinage

Upstyles

Celeste J. Adrete Innovations
HAIR: Tara Russell
MAKEUP: Sara Wayne
PHOTO: Taggart Winterhalter
for Purely Visual

Celeste J. Adrete Innovations
HAIR: Celeste J. Aldrete
MAKEUP: Sara Wayne
PHOTO: Taggart Winterhalter for Purely Visual

Upstyles

35

HAIR: Dean Roybal
MAKEUP: Lori Neapolitan
PHOTO: Michael S. Block

Celeste J. Adrete Innovations
HAIR: Tara Russell
MAKEUP: Sara Wayne
PHOTO: Taggart Winterhalter
for Purely Visual

Upstyles

BennieFactor Products
HAIR: Team BennieFactor
MAKEUP: Lesa Miller
PHOTO: Ed Brown

Pavé Nouveau
HAIR: Ashley Schmidt
MAKEUP: Sara Wayne
PHOTO: Taggart Winterhalter
for Purely Visual

Salon 56
HAIR: Gerine Coronado
MAKEUP: Gerine Coronado
PHOTO: Taggart Winterhalter
for Purely Visual

Upstyles

39

HAIR: Barbara Lhotan
MAKEUP: Barbara Lhotan
PHOTO: Keston Duke

Academy of Style
HAIR: Danielle Krohn
MAKEUP: Bethany Killingbeck
PHOTO: Alexandra Livesay

Planet Salon
HAIR: Angela Major
MAKEUP: Angela Major
PHOTO: Christy Elaine

Upstyles

41

Fantastic Sams-Chino, CA
HAIR: Crystal Pershing
PHOTO: Taggart Winterhalter
for Purely Visual

Fantastic Sams-Temecula, CA
HAIR: Ryan DiGregorio
MAKEUP: Jaime Queenin &
Sara Wayne
PHOTO: Taggart
Winterhalter
for Purely Visual

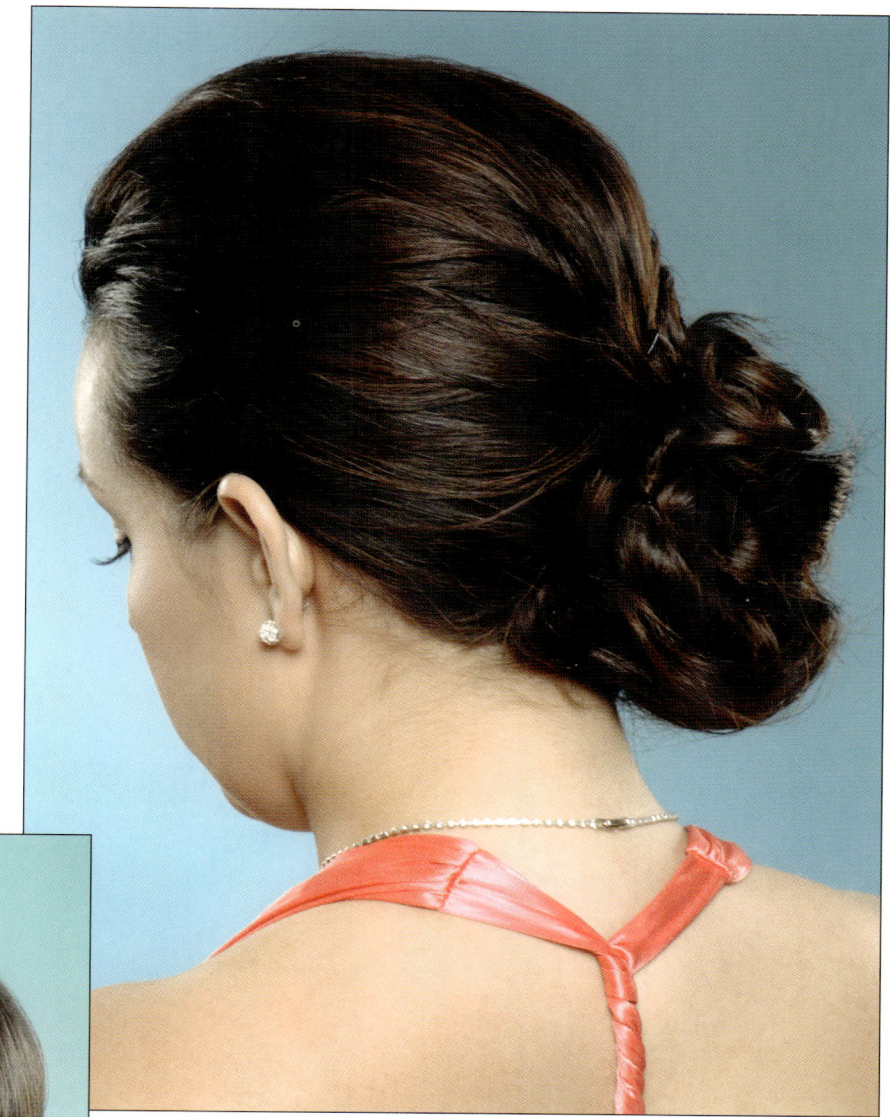

Fantastic Sams-Corona, CA
HAIR: Michelle Neto
PHOTO: Taggart Winterhalter
for Purely Visual

Fantastic Sams Riverside, CA
HAIR: Lily Dalou
PHOTO: Taggart Winterhalter for Purely Visual

Upstyles

Pavé Nouveau
HAIR: Ashley Schmidt
MAKEUP: Jaime Queenin
PHOTO: Taggart Winterhalter
for Purely Visual

Salon 56
HAIR: Stacy Klepach
MAKEUP: Stacy Klepach
PHOTO: Taggart Winterhalter for Purely Visual

Upstyles

Fantastic Sams Murrieta, CA
HAIR: Nina Serrano
PHOTO: Taggart Winterhalter for Purely Visual

Salon 56
HAIR: Kati Sartini
MAKEUP: Harold Morris
PHOTO: Taggart Winterhalter for Purely Visual

46

Fantastic Sams-Corona, CA
HAIR: Tannya Vasquez
PHOTO: Taggart Winterhalter for Purely Visual

Fantastic Sams-Norco, CA
HAIR: Linda Morrell
PHOTO: Taggart Winterhalter for Purely Visual

Upstyles

47

One Cut Above/Merle Norman
HAIR: Ann Cazzelle
MAKEUP: Vivian Gibson
PHOTO: Tony Thompsen

Angeleah's
HAIR: Angeleah Daidone
MAKEUP: Patricia Daidone
PHOTO: Angeleah Daidone

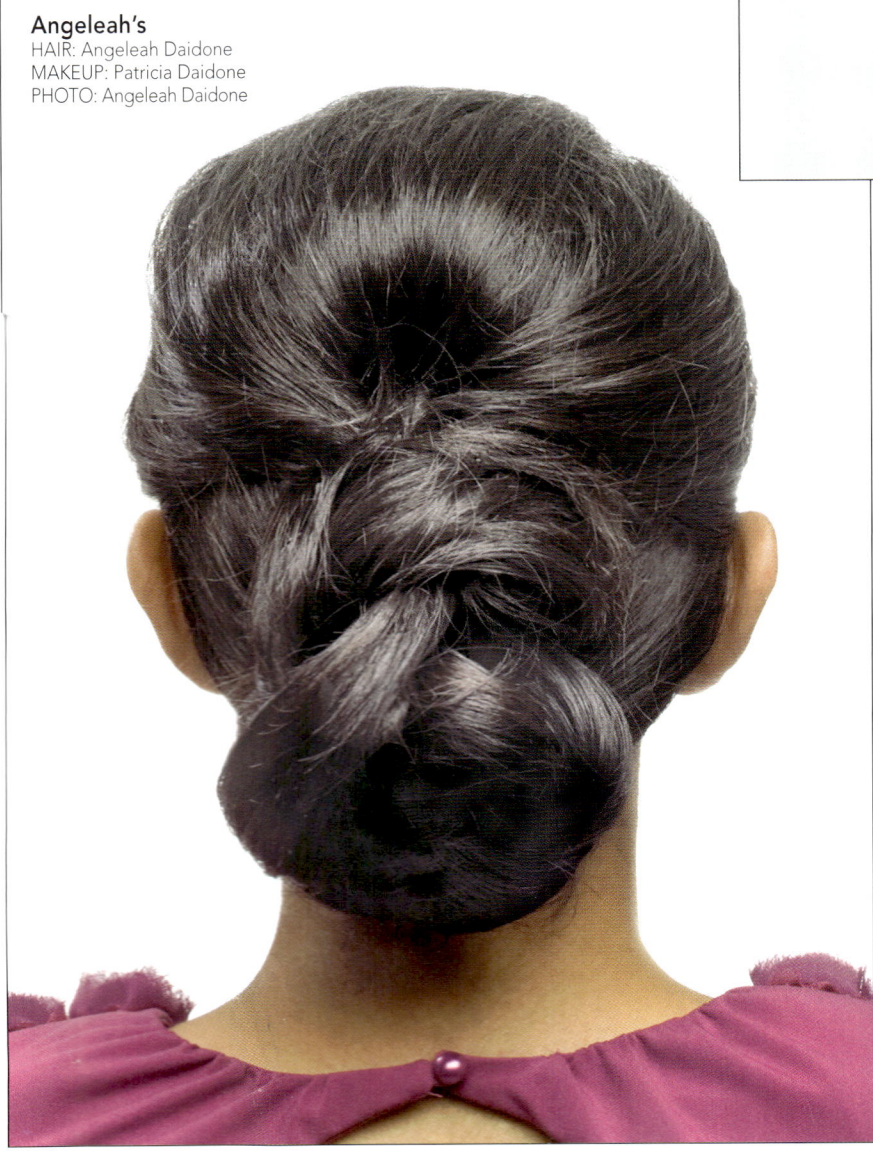

Upstyles

M-The Salon/MAKA Beauty Systems
HAIR: Robyn Rasmussen
MAKEUP: Mindy Hay
PHOTO: Matt Spencer

Grand Avenue Salon
HAIR: Manuel Mora
MAKEUP: Sara Wayne
PHOTO: Taggart Winterhalter for Purely Visual

Fantastic Sams-Murrieta, CA
HAIR: Heather Leseberg
PHOTO: Taggart Winterhalter
for Purely Visual

Upstyles

51

Fantastic Sams-Upland, CA
HAIR: Dany Nguon
PHOTO: Taggart Winterhalter
for Purely Visual

Fantastic Sams-Chino, CA
HAIR: Elia Munguia
PHOTO: Taggart Winterhalter
for Purely Visual

Fantastic Sams-Lake Elsinore, CA
HAIR: Rosalia Gauana
PHOTO: Taggart Winterhalter
for Purely Visual

Mosaic Day Spa & Salon
HAIR: Sandra Baliya
COLOR: Sandra Baliya
MAKEUP: Sandra Baliya
PHOTO: Jeff Tureaud

Upstyles

53

Special Effects Hair Design Studio
HAIR: Linda deBrauwer
COLOR: Jimmy de
MAKEUP: Linda deBrauwer
PHOTO: Jimmy de

Estilo Salon & Day Spa
HAIR: Jenny Raasch
MAKEUP: Sarah Kelley
PHOTO: Paul Bunkofske

Upstyles

55

BennieFactor Products
HAIR: Team BennieFactor
MAKEUP: Lesa Miller
PHOTO: Ed Brown

Estilo Salon & Day Spa
HAIR: Jenny Raasch
MAKEUP: Mallory Soda
PHOTO: Ket Quang

Estilo Salon & Day Spa
HAIR: Jenny Raasch
MAKEUP: Mallory Soda
PHOTO: Ket Quang

Upstyles

57

Carter T. Lund and Associates
HAIR: Carter T. Lund
MAKEUP: Jaime Queenin
PHOTO: Taggart Winterhalter
for Purely Visual

Rejuvenation Spa
HAIR: Megan Benson
MAKEUP: Megan Benson
PHOTO: Amy & Jennifer Johnson

élon Salon
HAIR: Repkna Hicks
PHOTO: Tom Carson

Special Effects Hair Design Studio
HAIR: Linda deBrauwer
COLOR: Jimmy de
MAKEUP: Linda deBrauwer
PHOTO: Jimmy de

Upstyles

**Fantastic Sams
Foothill Ranch, CA**
HAIR: Jennifer Pecbot
PHOTO: Taggart Winterhalter
for Purely Visual

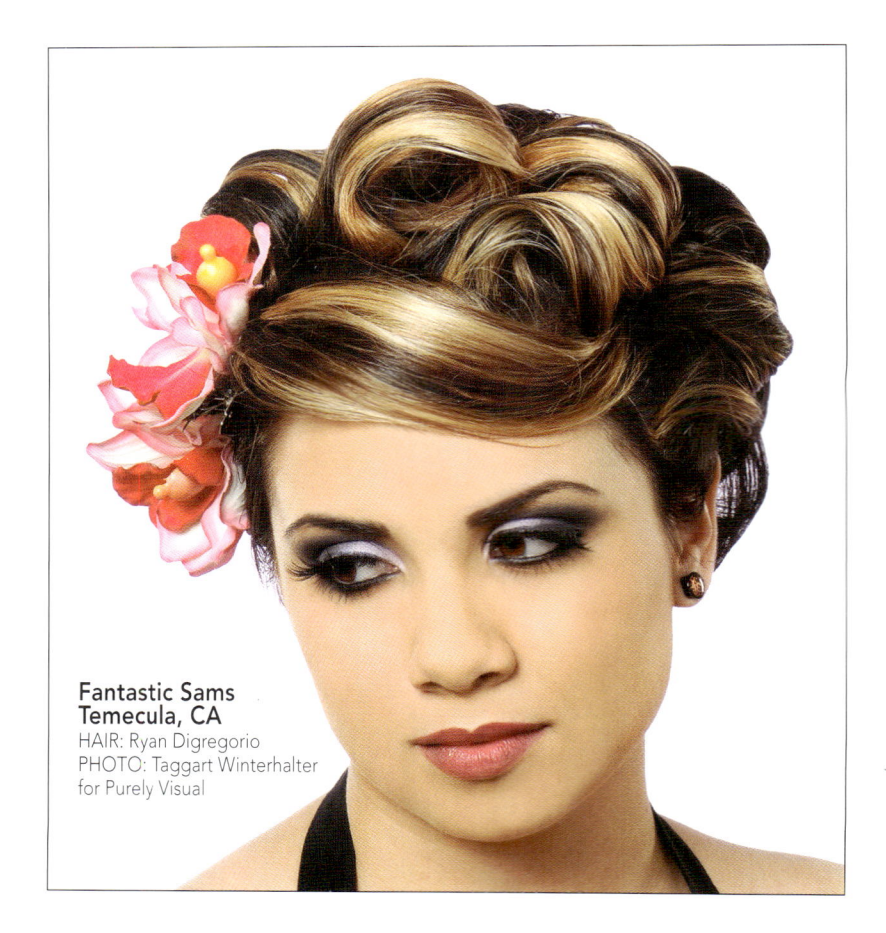

**Fantastic Sams
Temecula, CA**
HAIR: Ryan Digregorio
PHOTO: Taggart Winterhalter
for Purely Visual

Cloud 9 Salon
HAIR: Julie Marling
MAKEUP: April Stoner
PHOTO: Tom Carson

Upstyles

61

Anása Hair Studio
HAIR: Jennifer Foerster
MAKEUP: Jennifer Foerster
PHOTO: Taggart Winterhalter for Purely Visual

Fantastic Sams-Norco, CA
HAIR: Linda Morrell
PHOTO: Taggart Winterhalter for Purely Visual

Special Occasion Hair

**M-The Salon/
MAKA Beauty Systems**
HAIR: Kristin Garcia
MAKEUP: Mindy Hay
PHOTO: Matt Spencer

Fantastic Sams-San Pedro, CA
HAIR: Maria Medina
PHOTO: Taggart Winterhalter
for Purely Visual

PON International
HAIR: Tayja Avila
MAKEUP: Sara Wayne
PHOTO: Taggart
Winterhalter for
Purely Visual

64

So Cap USA
HAIR: Kathy Williams
MAKEUP: Bea Ross
PHOTO: Scott Bryant

Salon 56
HAIR: Maria Grijalva
MAKEUP: Jaime Queenin
PHOTO: Taggart Winterhalter
for Purely Visual

Special Occasion Hair

65

Fantastic Sams-Corona, CA
HAIR: Jacinda Higgins
PHOTO: Taggart Winterhalter
for Purely Visual

Special Occasion Hair

Special Effects Hair Design Studio
HAIR: Linda deBrauwer
COLOR: Jimmy de
MAKEUP: Linda deBrauwer
PHOTO: Jimmy de

So Cap USA
HAIR: Kathy Williams
COLOR: Kathy Williams
MAKEUP: Bea Ross
PHOTO: Scott Bryant

Pavé Nouveau
HAIR: Lauren McBride
MAKEUP: Jaime Queenin
PHOTO: Taggart Winterhalter for Purely Visual

Claudes Beautorium
HAIR: Leslie Dehner
MAKEUP: Leslie Dehner
PHOTO: Damon Smith

Pivot Point International
HAIR: Angelina Pasquet, Joakim Roos,
Tulio Talia, Martin Wenstel & Pascal Viton
MAKEUP: Carla Rep
PHOTO: Rob Peetoom

Special Occasion Hair

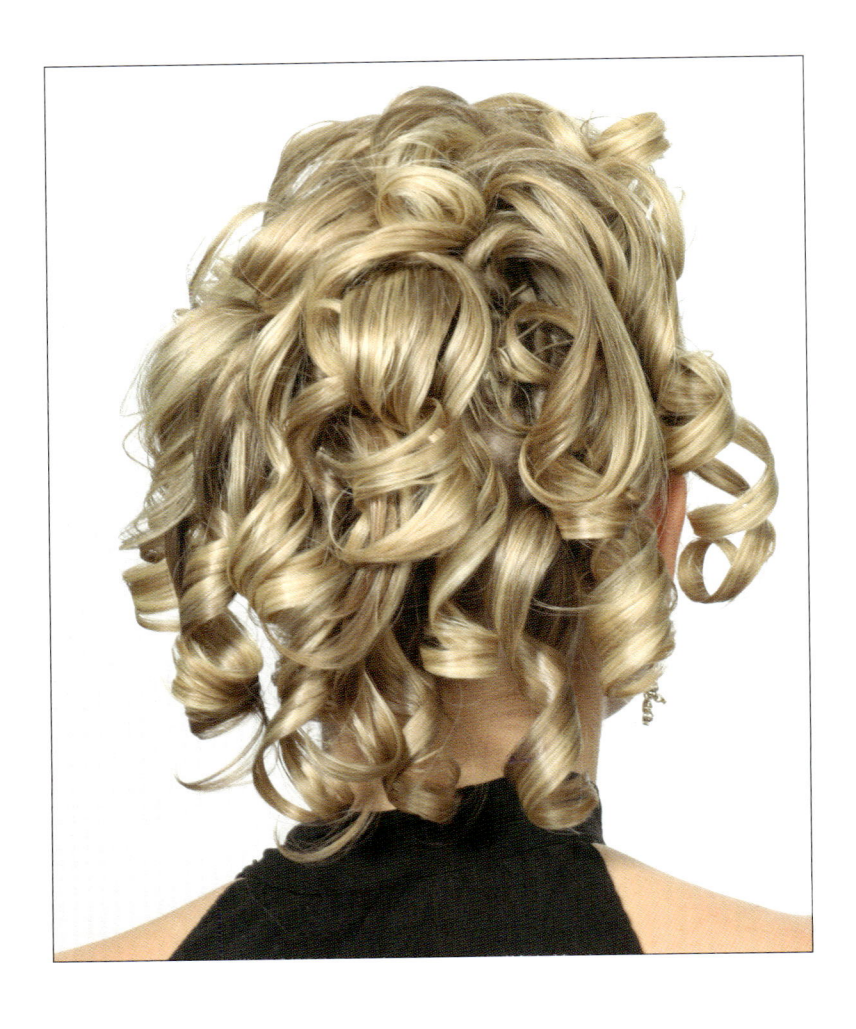

Ronnie Elias Salon
HAIR: Devin Simmons
COLOR: Devin Simmons
MAKEUP: Erin O'Halloram
PHOTO: Scott Bryant

Hair Xtreme Salon
HAIR: Kim West
COLOR: Kim West
MAKEUP: Karen Allyn
PHOTO: Scott Bryant

Hairlines Salon & Spa
HAIR: Stacy Kong
MAKEUP: Melissa Lizbinski
PHOTO: Thuat Kong

Tangles Salon
HAIR: Chase Williams
PHOTO: Tom Carson

Special Occasion Hair

71

Luca Bella Salon and Spa
HAIR: Kelly Meador
MAKEUP: JáNice Estrada
PHOTO: Taggart Winterhalter for Purely Visual

The Art of Hair Grand Salon
HAIR: Nicole Simmons
MAKEUP: Jamie Queenin
PHOTO: Taggart Winterhalter for Purely Visual

American Beauty Academy
HAIR: Holly Despain
MAKEUP: Holly Despain
PHOTO: Joe Putnam

Macy's Elizabeth Arden Salon
HAIR: Diana Colaizzi
PHOTO: David C. Barker

Special Occasion Hair

73

Eclips Salon & Day Spa
HAIR: Deborah Prizzia
COLOR: Deborah Prizzia
MAKEUP: Karlyn Cutsforth
PHOTO: Scott Bryant

Special Occasion Hair

Artistic Hair
HAIR: Laura Griffin
MAKEUP: Jamie Queenin
PHOTO: Taggart Winterhalter for Purely Visual

The Hair Loft
HAIR: Sharon LeFebvre
MAKEUP: Emily Redman
PHOTO: Artistic Images of Canton, LLC

TressAllure
HAIR: Alan Eaton

TressAllure
HAIR: Alan Eaton

TressAllure
HAIR: Alan Eaton

Special Occasion Hair

Level 7 Hair Design
HAIR: Trish Bagby
MAKEUP: Barbie Mercedes
PHOTO: Crae Clements

Fantastic Sams Corona, CA
HAIR: April Mead
PHOTO: Taggart Winterhalter for Purely Visual

77

Luca Bella Salon & Spa
HAIR: Jolene Phillips
MAKEUP: Jamie Queenin
PHOTO: Taggart Winterhalter
for Purely Visual

Special Occasion Hair

StevenMichael's
HAIR: Steven Aultman
MAKEUP: Jamie Queenin
PHOTO: Taggart Winterhalter
for Purely Visual

Art of Hair
HAIR: Nicole Martin
MAKEUP: Jamie Queenin
PHOTO: Taggart Winterhalter for Purely Visual

Martin Parsons
HAIR: Martin Parsons
MAKEUP: Cheryl Gushue
PHOTO: Dave Starrett
*Courtesy of Martin Parsons

Anása Hair Studio
HAIR: Angelina
MAKEUP: Jeanne Romano
PHOTO: Taggart Winterhalter for Purely Visual

Hairlines Salon & Spa
HAIR: Stacy Kong
MAKEUP: Melissa Lizbinski
PHOTO: Thuat Kong

Special Occasion Hair

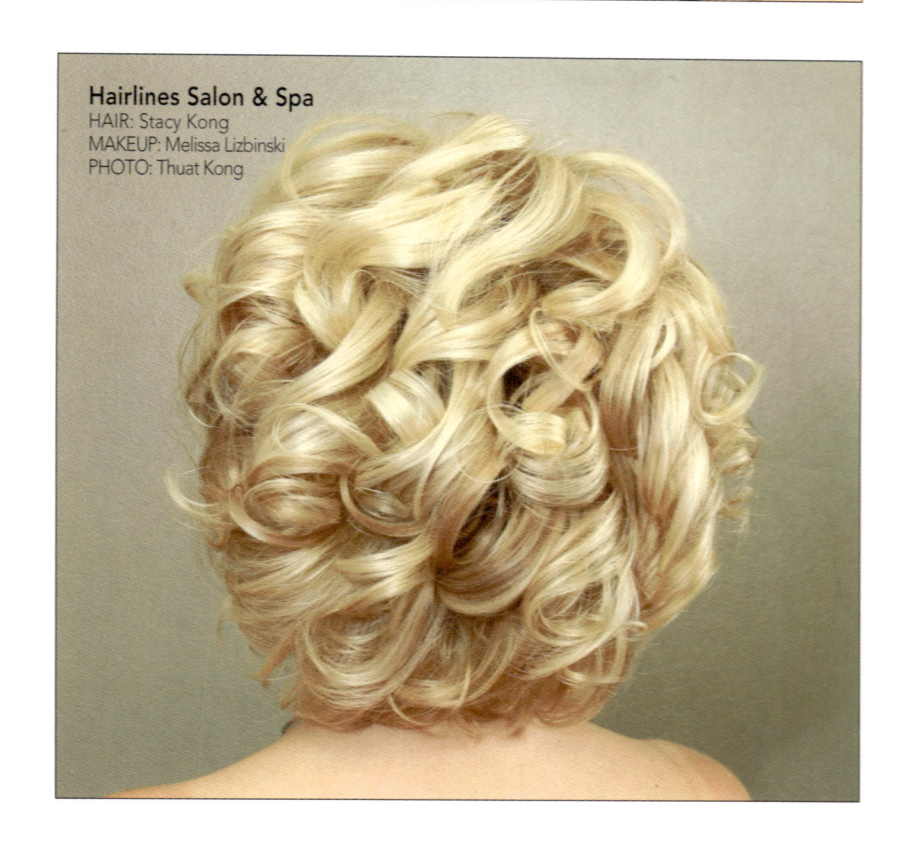

81

Fantastic Sams-Riverside, CA
HAIR: Amy Hunter
PHOTO: Taggart Winterhalter for Purely Visual

Art of Hair
HAIR: Nicole Martin
MAKEUP: Sara Wayne
PHOTO: Taggart Winterhalter for Purely Visual

Vizion Hair Salon
HAIR: Michele Saenz
MAKEUP: Sara Wayne
PHOTO: Taggart Winterhalter for Purely Visual

Special Occasion Hair

83

Rumors Salon and Spa
HAIR: Amber Nieckare
MAKEUP: Jennifer Schwartz
PHOTO: Denis J. Nally

Brittany's Spa Salon
HAIR: Brittany Molina
MAKEUP: Lillia Budnick
PHOTO: Steven Spoons

Special Occasion Hair

One Cut Above/Merle Norman
HAIR: Ann Cazzelle
MAKEUP: Vivian Gibson
PHOTO: Tony Thompsen

Salon 56
HAIR: Gerine Coronado
MAKEUP: Gerine Coronado
PHOTO: Taggart Winterhalter
for Purely Visual

Special Occasion Hair

Nicole Kidman
PHOTO: Kevin Winter
Getty Images Entertainment

Eva Longoria
PHOTO: Evan Agostini
Getty Images Entertainment

Haylie Duff
PHOTO: Stephen Shugerman
Getty Images Entertainment

Celebrity Upstyles

Barbara Mori
PHOTO: Sean Gallup
Getty Images Entertainment

Barbara Mori
PHOTO: Pascal Le Segretain
Getty Images Entertainment

Amanda Seyfried
PHOTO: Jason Merritt
Getty Images Entertainment

Amanda Seyfried
PHOTO: ROBYN BECK
AFP/Getty Images Entertainment

90

Kate Beckinsale
PHOTO: Eric Ryan
Getty Images Entertainment

Kate Beckinsale
PHOTO: Dave M. Benett
Getty Images Entertainment

Jessica Alba
PHOTO: Frazer Harrison
Getty Images Entertainment

Jessica Alba
PHOTO: Frazer Harrison
Getty Images Entertainment

Celebrity Upstyles

Kim Kardashian
PHOTO: Jason Merritt
Getty Images Entertainment

Kim Kardashian
PHOTO: Steve Granitz
WireImage

Kim Kardashian
PHOTO: Steve Granitz
WireImage

Nicollette Sheridan
PHOTO: Kevin Winter
Getty Images Entertainment

Nicollette Sheridan
PHOTO: Kevin Winter
Getty Images Entertainment

Christina Ricci
PHOTO: Jean Baptiste Lacroix
WireImage

Christina Ricci
PHOTO: Alberto E. Rodriguez
Getty Images Entertainment

Celebrity Upstyles

Kristen Bell
PHOTO: Jason Merritt
Getty Images Entertainment

Kristen Bell
PHOTO: Steve Granitz
WireImage

Angelina Jolie
PHOTO: Jun Sato
WireImage

Christina Aguilera
PHOTO: Jason Merritt
Getty Images Entertainment

Celebrity Upstyles

95

INSPIRE
HAIR FASHION FOR SALON CLIENTS
INDEX VOLUME SEVENTY EIGHT

Salon	Photographer	Page
Academy of Style	Alexandra Livesay	41
Affinage	Paul Sargaison for Affinage	33
American Beauty Academy	Joe Putman	73
Anása Hair Studio	Taggart Winterhalter for Purely Visual	62,81
Angeleah's	Angeleah Diadone	24,48
Art of Hair	Taggart Winterhalter for Purely Visual	8,13,80,82
Artistic Hair	Taggart Winterhalter for Purely Visual	75
Barbara Lhotan	Kestin Duke	40
BennieFactor Products	Ed Brown	38,56
Bristles & Shears	Ed Soloman	76
Brittany's Spa Salon	Steven Spoons	85
Carter T. Lund and Associates	Taggart Winterhalter for Purely Visual	58
Celeste J. Adrete Innovations	Taggart Winterhalter for Purely Visual	34,35,37
Claudes Beautorium	Damon Smith	68
Cloud 9 Salon	Tom Carson	61
Cuttin Inn Salon & Spa	Taggart Winterhalter for Purely Visual	29
David Douglas Salon and Spa	Taggart Winterhalter for Purely Visual	9
Dean Roybal	Michael S. Block	9,31,36
Eclips Salon & Day Spa	Scott Bryant	74
élon Salon	Tom Carson	59
Estilo Salon & Day Spa	Paul Bunkofske	55
Estilo Salon & Day Spa	Ket Quang	57
Fantastic Sams-Chino, CA	Taggart Winterhalter for Purely Visual	42,52
Fantastic Sams-Corona, CA	Taggart Winterhalter for Purely Visual	43,47,66,77
Fantastic Sams-Foothill Ranch, CA	Taggart Winterhalter for Purely Visual	60
Fantastic Sams-Hungtington Beach, CA	Taggart Winterhalter for Purely Visual	14,15,17
Fantastic Sams-Lake Elsinore, CA	Taggart Winterhalter for Purely Visual	53
Fantastic Sams-Murrieta, CA	Taggart Winterhalter for Purely Visual	45,51
Fantastic Sams-Norco, CA	Taggart Winterhalter for Purely Visual	47,62
Fantastic Sams-Rancho Cucamonga, CA	Taggart Winterhalter for Purely Visual	14
Fantastic Sams-Riverside, CA	Taggart Winterhalter for Purely Visual	43,82
Fantastic Sams-San Pedro, CA	Taggart Winterhalter for Purely Visual	54
Fantastic Sams-Temecula, CA	Taggart Winterhalter for Purely Visual	42,60
Fantastic Sams-Upland, CA	Taggart Winterhalter for Purely Visual	52
Grand Avenue Salon	Taggart Winterhalter for Purely Visual	50
Hair International	Kristin Szczerbik	17
Hair Xtreme Salon	Scott Bryant	70
Hairlines Salon & Spa	Thuat Kong	71,81
John Amico Haircare & Jalyd Haircolor Parkview Shear Perfection	Scott Bryant	22
Level 7 Hair Design	Crae Clements	77
Luca Bella Salon and Spa	Taggart Winterhalter for Purely Visual	72,78
Macy's Elizabeth Arden Salon	David C. Barker	73
*Martin Parsons	Dave Starrett	29,80
Mosaic Day Spa & Salon	Jeff Tureaud	23,53
M-The Salon/MAKA Beauty Systems	Matt Spencer	26,49,63
Navii Salon Spa	Jean Sweet	4,5,6,10
One Cut Above/Merle Norman	Tony Thompsen	48,86
Pavé Nouveau	Taggart Winterhalter for Purely Visual	12,27,28,30,32,39,44,68
Pivot Point International	Rob Peetoom	69
Planet Salon	Christy Elaine	41
PON International	Taggart Winterhalter for Purely Visual	64
Rejuvenation Spa	Amy & Jennifer Johnson	58
Ronnie Elias Salon	Scott Bryant	70
Rumors Salon and Spa	Denis J. Nally	20,84
Salon 56	Taggart Winterhalter for Purely Visual	7,11,39,45,46,65,87
Salon De Christe'	Heather Ramirez	18
Salon Secrets Spa & Wellness Retreat	Scott Bryant	22
Salon Tekniques	Scott Bryant	18
So Cap USA	Scott Bryant	65,67
Special Effects Hair Design Studio	Jimmy de	54,59,67
StevenMichael's	Taggart Winterhalter for Purely Visual	79
Tangles Salon	Tom Carson	71
The Art of Hair	Taggart Winterhalter for Purely Visual	31
The Art of Hair Grand Salon	Taggart Winterhalter for Purely Visual	72
The Hair Loft	Artistic Images of Canton, LLC	23,75
The Hair Station	Terri Feldpausch	13
The Salon Professionals	Tina VanDerhoof	25
TressAllure		76
Updo's Studio	Still Shots Photography	19
Visible Changes	Dan Carter	21
Vizion Hair Salon	Taggart Winterhalter for Purely Visual	83
	Kevin Winter/Getty Images Entertainment	88,93
	Evan Agostini/Getty Images Entertainment	89
	Stephan Shugerman/Getty Images Entertainment	89
	Pascal Le Segretain/Getty Images Entertainment	90
	Sean Gallup/Getty Images Entertainment	90
	Frazer Harrison/Getty Images Entertainment	90,91
	Jason Merritt/Getty Images Entertainment	90,92,94,95
	Dave M. Benett/Getty Images Entertainment	91
	Venturelli/WireImage	91
	Steve Granitz/WireImage	92,94
	Jean Baptise Lacroix/WireImage	93
	Alberto E. Rodriguez/Getty Images Entertainment	93
	Jun Sato/WireImage	94

*Courtesy of Martin Parsons
Publisher/CEO: Deborah Carver • Managing Director: Sheryl Lenzkes • Art Director: Michael Block
To Contact Us: Creative Age Communications • 7628 Densmore Avenue, Van Nuys, California 91406-2042 • PH 800.634.8500 • FAX 818.782.7450
Interested in getting published . . . go to inspirebooks.com to download submission forms and information